The Midwife's Apprentice

L-I-T *Guide*

Literature In Teaching

By Karen Cushman

A Study Guide for Grades 5 to 10
Prepared by Charlotte S. Jaffe and Barbara T. Doherty
Illustrated by Koryn Agnello

The purchase of this book entitles the individual
teacher to reproduce copies of the student pages for use
in his or her classroom exclusively. The reproduction
of any part of the work for an entire school or school
system or for commercial use is prohibited.

ISBN 1-56644-015-7

© 1998 Educational Impressions, Inc., Hawthorne, NJ

EDUCATIONAL IMPRESSIONS, INC.
Hawthorne, NJ 07507

Printed in the United States of America.

This study guide is based on the book *The Midwife's Apprentice:*
  Copyright 1995 by Karen Cushman
  Published by Clarion Books: New York

The Midwife's Apprentice

Written by Karen Cushman

STORY SUMMARY

In the early fourteenth century in England, a girl known only as Brat wandered into a small village. She went to sleep in a dung heap, the only warm place she could find. Jane the Midwife awakened her and called her Beetle, for the girl reminded her of a dung beetle burrowed in the heap. Jane offered to give her food and a place to stay in exchange for work.

Although Beetle's life was not as harsh as before, there was little time for enjoyment—that is, until Jane broke her ankle. Unable to go herself, Jane told Beetle to go to the Saint Swithin's Day Fair in her place. On her own, Beetle was able to enjoy the wondrous goings-on. Given a comb by a generous merchant, she put it through her hair, revealing her fine curls. Imagine her surprise when she was then mistaken for a girl named Alyce—a girl who could read! Liking the feeling, she decided to take the name as her own.

One night the midwife left Alyce alone with the Bailiff's wife, who was about to give birth. Although the midwife had believed that the baby would not be born alive, Alyce successfully delivered the child. The experience filled her with pride and satisfaction. From then on Alyce secretly watched as the midwife worked, trying to learn as much as she could.

When the sister of the Bailiff's wife was about to give birth, she summoned Alyce to help. Believing she was skilled enough to handle the situation, Alyce went to the woman; however, she was too inexperienced and could not care for the woman on her own. The real midwife had to be called.

Ashamed, Alyce ran away, taking her cat, Purr, with her. They wandered until they came to an inn, where Alyce again bargained for a place to sleep and food to eat in exchange for work. Alyce proved so helpful that the innkeeper asked her to stay. While she was there, she met many new people, including the scholarly Magister Reese, who taught her to read.

Time passed, and one afternoon, having heard Alyce was there, Jane the Midwife visited the inn. She engaged Magister Reese in conversation. Alyce hid and listened carefully to what they said. She heard Jane tell him that Alyce was not what she needed—not because she was incompetent, but because she gave up when things went wrong.

One evening a party of riders arrived at the inn. Among them were a prosperous-looking man and his wife, who was in great pain—supposedly with a stomach worm. When it was determined that the woman was, in fact, about to give birth, Alyce reluctantly agreed to help. She successfully delivered a healthy baby boy.

Certain of what she wanted to do with her life, Alyce left the inn with Purr and returned to the village. She headed straight for the midwife's cottage. At first, Jane wouldn't let her in. Alyce soon convinced her, however, that she was ready to persist in her goal. She would not give up again.

Meet the Author
Karen Cushman

Karen Cushman didn't start her career until she was fifty years old. "I'm a late bloomer," she says with a laugh. Born in Chicago, Illinois, she attended college and graduate school, receiving an M.A. in human behavior and museum studies. Encouraged by her love for history, Cushman decided to set her first novel, *Catherine, Called Birdy,* in medieval England.

Before she began her writing, she read other young-adult historical novels and was impressed by their "simple and polished prose." Cushman sought out writing advice from other professionals and was told to write from her heart. Her job as teacher of museum studies at Kennedy University in California provided her with background materials to use in her novel.

At first, Cushman was not encouraged by the reaction to her manuscript. "That's interesting, but it will never sell," she was told. Luckily, the author did not give up. Three years later, with the help of a supportive editor, her first novel was published. It received the 1995 Newbery Honor Award, the ALA Notable Children's Book Award, and the Golden Kite Award, among others. Her next novel, *The Midwife's Apprentice,* won the prestigious Newbery Medal. In both novels, the heroines are adolescent girls, and life in medieval England is seen through their eyes.

Karen Cushman lives in Oakland, California, with her husband who writes books about psychology. They have one daughter, Leah. Cushman's latest novel is *The Ballad of Lucy Whipple,* another coming-of-age book. It is set in the California Gold Rush era. The author is delighted with her new writing career and urges new and would-be writers , "Go with your passion."

Vocabulary
Chapter One: *The Dung Heap*

Use the words in the box to complete the sentences. You may need to use your dictionary.

apprentice	bailiff	burrowed	dung	fragrant	heedless
ill-used	lest	moiling	muck	rank	reeked
scavenged	snug	stench	tormented	toddled	wimple

1. The sweepings from the stable were added to the _______________ pile.

2. _______________ herbs made the room smell wonderful.

3. _______________ of the warning, Brad dove into the shallow water of the pool.

4. Lady Catherine's _______________ hid her beautiful thick hair.

5. The mosquitoes _______________ the campers all night.

6. Although he is only a(n) _______________, Michael has learned many carpentry skills.

7. The wind carried the _______________ of the landfill away from us.

8. We _______________ through the shipwreck for anything useful.

9. After Andrew's encounter with the skunk, his clothing _______________ from the spray.

10. The baby _______________ on unsure legs to her mother's arms.

11. The sheriff sent the _______________ to collect the farmers' rents.

12. The _______________ of the swamp was _______________and sticky.

13. The cottages seemed cozy and _______________ against the autumn chill.

14. The _______________ horse ran away from its cruel owner.

Three of the vocabulary words were not used. Write an original sentence using each of those words.

____

____

____

Comprehension and Discussion Questions
Chapter One: *The Dung Heap*

Answer the following questions in complete sentence form. Give examples from the story to support your response.

1. Describe Brat's outlook on life.

____

____

____

____

2. Why was the midwife willing to give Brat some food?

____

____

____

____

3. Why did the woman call the girl Beetle?

____

____

____

____

4. How did the girl compare her new place to sleep with the dung heap? How would you feel in her place?

____

____

____

____

Vocabulary
Chapter Two: *The Cat*

Match the vocabulary words on the left to the definitions on the right. Place the correct letter on each line.

____	1. aloft	A.	to one side; crooked
____	2. avoided	B.	playful; lively
____	3. bedeviled	C.	glowing
____	4. burrs	D.	motivate; influence
____	5. cockeyed	E.	an obnoxious person
____	6. frisky	F.	giving reluctantly; not generous
____	7. generous	G.	rough, prickly envelopes of fruit
____	8. gleaming	H.	stem end of grasses left in ground after harvesting
____	9. hunched	I.	high up; on top of
____	10. inspire	J.	liberal in sharing
____	11. scurrying	K.	a kind of tree with narrow, sometimes trailing, leaves
____	12. sod	L.	kept away from
____	13. stingy	M.	scampering
____	14. stubble	N.	tormented
____	15. willow	O.	bent or drawn up into a hump

Choose three of the vocabulary words from the first part of this activity. Use each in an original sentence.

____

____

____

Comprehension and Discussion Questions
Chapter Two: *The Cat*

Answer the following questions in complete sentence form. Give examples from the story to support your response.

1. Why did Beetle curse the cat when she was worried that it might drown?

____

____

____

2. Why did Beetle keep walking away and then returning to the cat after she pulled it out of the pond?

____

____

____

3. Why did Beetle try so hard to save the cat's life?

____

____

____

4. Why didn't Beetle celebrate Lady Day with the other villagers?

____

____

____

Vocabulary
Chapter Three: *The Midwife*

Part One: Choose the word or phrase in each set that is **most like** the first word in meaning.

1. **furrows:**   dots   rows   shadows

2. **endured:**   suffered   forgot   started

3. **columbine:**   buttercup   orange   daisy

4. **compassion:**   ignorance   commence   sympathy

5. **curdled:**   strained   spotted   coagulated

6. **flask:**   bottle   flare   conceal

7. **plough:**   turn over   replace   break

Part Two: Choose the word in each set that is **most unlike** the first word in meaning.

1. **accompanied:**   escorted   attended   abandoned

2. **encourage:**   urge   discourage   motivate

3. **haggling:**   bargaining   agreeing   arguing

4. **mumbled**   muttered   grumbled   articulated

5. **sowing:**   harvesting   scattering   spreading

6. **stanching:**   starting   halting   stopping

7. **sympathy:**   loyalty   understanding   insensitivity

 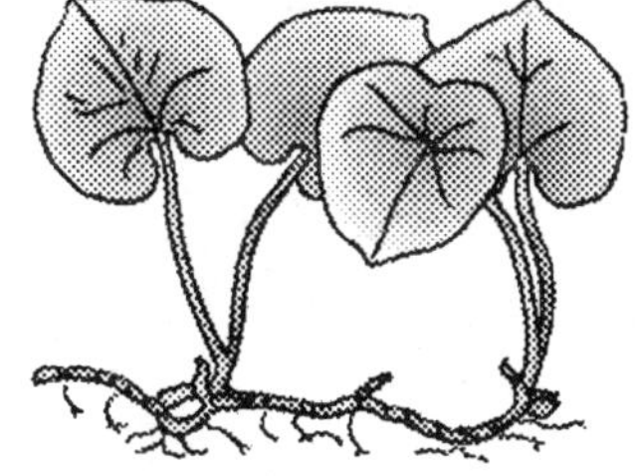 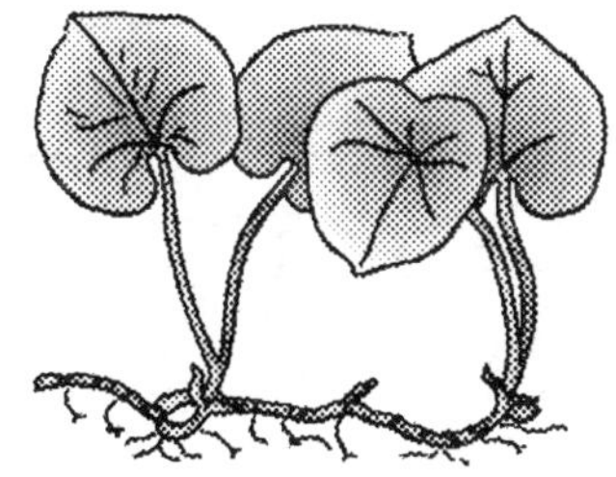

Comprehension and Discussion Questions
Chapter Three: *The Midwife*

Answer the following questions in complete sentence form. Give examples from the story to support your response.

1. What qualified Jane to be the midwife? Evaluate her credentials.

____

____

____

2. Why was the midwife willing to have Beetle as her apprentice? Why was Beetle willing to have Jane treat her so meanly?

____

____

____

3. Why did Beetle fear Jane Sharp might be a witch?

____

____

____

4. What did Beetle learn about herself by the end of this chapter?

____

____

____

Vocabulary
Chapter Four: *The Miller's Wife*

Use your dictionary to define the following words as they are used in this chapter.

1. **breeches:** ____

2. **chamber pot:** ____

3. **demons:** ____

4. **dwelling:** ____

5. **erupted:** ____

6. **loft:** ____

7. **luxurious:** ____

8. **nettle:** ____

9. **stalked:** ____

10. **thrust:** ____

11. **tot:** ____

12. **turmoil:** ____

Choose three vocabulary words from the first part of this activity. Use those words to build word webs. Place one vocabulary word in each circle. Then fill in the blanks with words that are related to the center word. Stretch your imagination and try to think of some unusual connections. An example is given.

Comprehension and Discussion Questions
Chapter Four: *The Miller's Wife*

Answer the following questions in complete sentence form. Give examples from the story to support your response.

1. Where was all the extra bread coming from?

____

____

____

____

2. Why was Beetle confused by the midwife's behavior? Did Beetle have reason to be confused?

____

____

____

____

3. Under different circumstances Beetle would have enjoyed going to the miller's house. Explain.

____

____

____

____

4. While at the Miller's house, Beetle felt like she was in Hell. Why?

____

____

____

____

Vocabulary
Chapter Five: *The Merchant*

Match the vocabulary words on the left to the definitions on the right. Place the correct letter on each line.

_____	1. abbey	A. lively; quick
_____	2. accomplish	B. food container
_____	3. brisk	C. wandered
_____	4. bronze	D. effect; result
_____	5. dire	E. irreverent statements using name of God
_____	6. embroidery	F. jobs; chores
_____	7. fancy	G. calamitous; having terrible consequences
_____	8. flax	H. supplies
_____	9. consequence	I. to fill or complete again
_____	10. laden	J. monastery; convent
_____	11. meandered	K. fortune teller
_____	12. oaths	L. a group of twenty
_____	13. ranting	M. a liking
_____	14. replenish	N. to get; to acquire
_____	15. score	O. fulfill; complete
_____	16. secure	P. earnestness; seriousness
_____	17. solemnity	Q. process of decorating with needlework
_____	18. soothsayer	R. various; miscellaneous
_____	19. stores	S. an alloy of copper and tin
_____	20. sundry	T. plant that yields linen
_____	21. tasks	U. talking loudly and wildly
_____	22. trough	V. burdened with

Write three sentences about something you might see or do at a fair. (Have you ever attended a "Renaissance" or "Medieval" Fair?)

____

____

____

Comprehension and Discussion Questions
Chapter Five: *The Merchant*

Answer the following questions in complete sentence form. Give examples from the story to support your response.

1. Although she had been to others in the past, Beetle wanted badly to go to this fair. Explain why.

____

____

____

____

2. How did Beetle know that this fair was important to Jane?

____

____

____

____

3. Explain why Beetle went to the fair instead of Jane.

____

____

____

____

4. Beetle enjoyed the wondrous things she saw at the fair. What else happened to make Beetle think that it had been a wonderful day? What important decision did she make as a result?

____

____

____

Vocabulary
Chapter Six: *The Naming*

Use your dictionary to define the following words as they are used in this chapter.

1. **daft:** ____

2. **gorm:** ____

3. **floundering:** _______________________________________

4. **hobbling:** ____

5. **lardy:** ____

6. **lentil:** ____

7. **occasional:** ____

8. **pluck:** ____

9. **rustled:** ____

10. **sheaves:** ____

11. **sputtering:** ____

12. **waddled:** ____

Create a Word-Search Puzzle

Use the vocabulary words from the first part of this activity to create a Word-Search Puzzle in the grid. Exchange with classmates to solve.

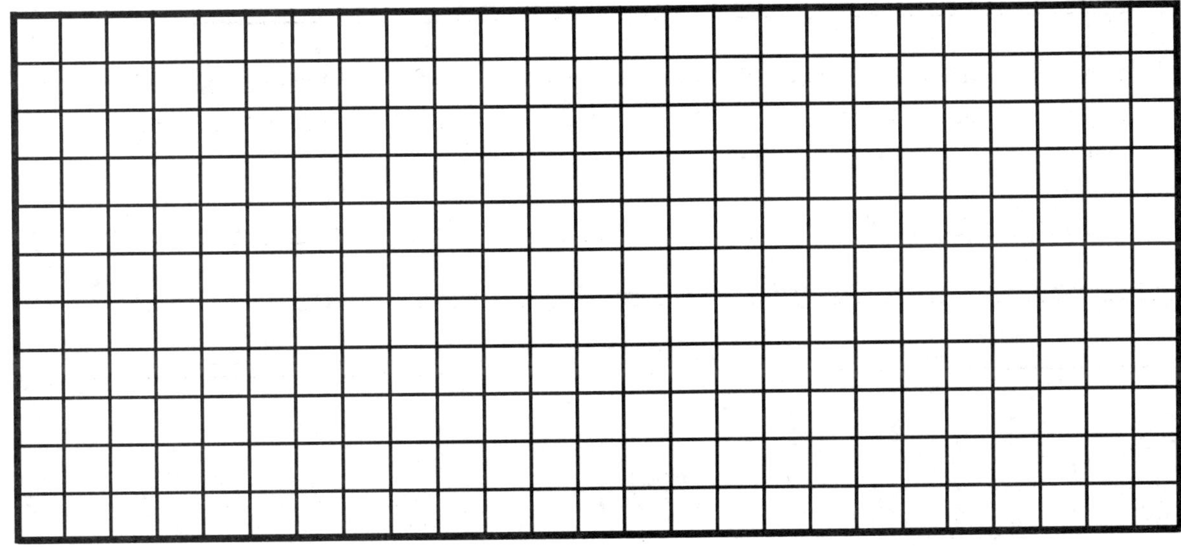

Comprehension and Discussion Questions
Chapter Six: *The Naming*

Answer the following questions in complete sentence form. Give examples from the story to support your response.

1. Why was Alyce out of Jane's sight and free to relax?

____

____

____

____

2. How did the cat get its name? Can you offer a better way of deciding on a pet's name?

____

____

____

____

3. What did Alyce do that earned her the respect of Will Russet?

____

____

____

____

4. How do we know that Alyce wasn't boastful? Do you think she was brave?

____

____

____

____

Vocabulary
Chapter Seven: *The Devil*

Use the words in the box to complete the sentences. You may need to use your dictionary.

breeches   delicate   dewclaws   fared   fetch

flung   gluttony   haymow   idle

incautious   paternosters   taunting   wag   weasel

1. Sally offered to ________________ the eggs from the hen house.

2. After the ________________ of the feast, everyone slept.

3. The area ________________ better than expected when the storm struck.

4. He recited the ________________ with his evening prayers.

5. Eggs have ________________ shells.

6. Alyce didn't like to be teased, but she learned to put up with the ________________.

7. There was only one ________________ hour in the hectic schedule.

8. A(n) ________________ is an enemy of a chicken farmer.

9. Speaking before thinking is a(n) ________________ habit.

10. The ________________ of some breeds of dogs are removed by veterinarians.

11. Robert got cold quickly because of his wet ________________ and jacket.

12. Alyce ________________ the packet as far as she could.

13. The lost child was found sleeping safely in the ________________.

14. Will listened to the rapid chatter; he soon became bored with the ________________.

Three of the vocabulary words were not used. Write an original sentence using each of those words.

____

____

____

____

Comprehension and Discussion Questions
Chapter Seven: *The Devil*

Answer the following questions in complete sentence form. Give examples from the story to support your response.

1. Explain how it was possible for Alyce to fool the villagers into believing that the devil was among them.

____

____

____

____

2. How did the "devil" choose whom to visit? Why, do you think, did Alyce spare the midwife?

____

____

____

____

3. How were crimes dealt with during this time in history? Give examples.

____

____

____

____

4. What became of the carved wooden blocks Alyce threw into the river?

____

____

____

____

Vocabulary
Chapter Eight: *The Twins*

Read each clue and find the answer in the box. Then use the letters above the numbered spaces to decipher the secret message.

accustomed bounty cautiously croon

fermenting gravel lout mellow mutton muck

nuzzling parsnips quarrying scrambled tart

1. climbed or ran in a quick, confused way
      __ __ __ __ __ __ __ __
       9   1   6

2. forming of alcohol from sugar
      __ __ __ __ __ __ __ __ __ __
        2   8

3. root vegetables similar to carrots
      __ __ __ __ __ __ __ __
       13

4. touching with the nose
      __ __ __ __ __ __ __ __
           5

5. a bit sour
      __ __ __ __
     4

6. small pieces of rock and pebbles
      __ __ __ __ __ __
           3 14

7. familiar with
      __ __ __ __ __ __ __ __ __ __
                11 12

8. with care
      __ __ __ __ __ __ __ __ __ __
     16 10   15

9. something given generously, a reward
      __ __ __ __ __ __
     7

10. tender and sweet
      __ __ __ __ __ __
       17

__ __ __ __ __ __   __ __ __ __ __ __
1 2 3 4 5 6   7 8 9 10 11 12

__ __ __ __ __
13 14 15 16 17

Three of the vocabulary words were not used. Write an original sentence using each of those words.

____

____

____

       The Midwife's Apprentice 19

Comprehension and Discussion Questions
Chapter Eight: *The Twins*

Answer the following questions in complete sentence form. Give examples from the story to support your response.

1. What made Alyce decide to help Will's cow deliver her calves?

____

____

____

____

2. How did Alyce's helping Will get her into trouble with Jane?

____

____

____

____

3. How do we know that the villagers were beginning to respect Alyce?

____

____

____

____

4. Why, do you suppose, did Alyce refuse to take the credit and to keep the payments?

____

____

____

____

Vocabulary
Chapter Nine: *The Bailiff's Wife's Baby*

Read each sentence. Then circle the most appropriate definition for the word printed in bold as it is used in that sentence.

1. Jane **bade** Michael to fill all of the baskets.

        paid for   ordered   dreamt

2. Sarah **bustled** around the stage!

    cautiously moved about   moved about busily   moved about quietly

3. Patrice treated her neighbor with **courtesy.**

        patience   charity   respect

4. She **flailed** her arms trying to get their attention.

        raised   swung   banged

5. From inside the closet, the **mewling** continued.

        whimpering   sniffling   humming

6. The **revelers** returned home at midnight.

        emergency team   party-goers   parents

7. Everyone was convinced that the medicine was really a **sham.**

        trick   herb   poison

8. Andrew **soothed** his mother's fears.

        disliked   compounded   comforted

9. The villagers **thrashed** the wheat all day before the rain came.

        indulged   beat   planted

10. The **viper** was found on the floor of the barn.

        cutting tool   small mammal   poisonous snake

If you could speak to Alyce now, what would you say? Use some vocabulary words from the first part of this activity.

____

____

____

Comprehension and Discussion Questions
Chapter Nine: *The Bailiff's Wife's Baby*

Answer the following questions in complete sentence form. Give examples from the story to support your response.

1. How did Alyce persuade the boys to stop teasing the cat?

____

____

____

____

2. Evaluate Jane's decision to leave the bailiff's wife to go to the manor.

____

____

____

____

3. How did Alyce make up for not knowing all of the magic and spells to help Joan?

____

____

____

____

4. What new feelings did Alyce experience as a result of helping the bailiff's wife? How did she express these feelings?

____

____

____

____

Vocabulary
Chapter Ten: *The Boy*

Use the words in the box to complete the sentences. You may need to use your dictionary.

manor   tunic   threshing   sprawled   summoned

reluctant   leeks   anise   contractions   runt   mallows

pursued   startled   huddled   hermit   abundant

1. Because there was a(n) _______________ supply of food, we all had plenty to eat.

2. The woman's _______________ was worn over a skirt.

3. My dog and cat _______________ close to each other in front of the warm fireplace.

4. The police officer _______________ the robber until he was finally captured.

5. We all _______________ on the beach under the big sun umbrellas.

6. I was _______________ to attend the outdoor concert because of a rainy forecast.

7. The lord and lady lived in a _______________ on the hillside.

8. The expectant mother felt the _______________ strengthen prior to the baby's birth.

9. After the auto accident, we quickly _______________ help.

10. The farmer hired workers to help with the _______________.

11. A loud sound _______________ the young child, and he began to cry.

12. Because he preferred to be alone, the _______________ lived in a remote area.

13. The _______________ seed is often used as a flavoring in cooking or as a medicine.

14. The juice of _______________ and _______________ shortened a woman's labor.

15. No one wanted to buy the _______________ of the litter because he was so small.

Choose three of the vocabulary words from the first part of the activity. Write an original sentence for each.

____

____

____

____

Comprehension and Discussion Questions
Chapter Ten: *The Boy*

Answer the following questions in complete sentence form. Give examples from the story to support your response.

1. How did Alyce prepare herself to be a midwife?

____

____

____

____

2. What helpful discoveries did Alyce make after observing the midwife in action? Which do you think was the most unusual?

____

____

____

____

3. Why did Alyce say to the boy, "Everybody is somebody and so are you"? How might this statement help him?

____

____

____

____

4. How did Runt become Edward?

____

____

____

____

Vocabulary
Chapter Eleven: *The Leaving*

Match the vocabulary words on the left to the definitions on the right. Place the correct letter on each line.

_____	1. bellowed	A. great disorder; confusion
_____	2. birch	B. pushed slightly
_____	3. chaos	C. small outhouse toilet
_____	4. comfrey	D. relieved; cured
_____	5. crisp	E. spoke incoherently
_____	6. nudged	F. killed
_____	7. privies	G. a slender, hardy tree with a smooth bark
_____	8. quivered	H. brisk; invigorating
_____	9. remedied	I. victorious
_____	10. sensations	J. shouted loudly
_____	11. slaughtered	K. feelings; perceptions
_____	12. spluttered	L. shook; trembled
_____	13. treachery	M. a bristly plant with different colored leaves
_____	14. triumphant	N. deceit; breaking of faith
_____	15. wail	O. to cry; to grieve out loud

Thinking Back

Tell about a time in your life when you suffered from a failure. Perhaps you didn't make the team, achieve a desired grade, win an award, etc. Use vocabulary words from Chapters Ten and Eleven in your story.

____

____

____

____

____

Comprehension and Discussion Questions
Chapter Eleven: *The Leaving*

Answer the following questions in complete sentence form. Give examples from the story to support your response.

1. Explain why Matthew Blunt asked for Alyce's help and not Jane's.

\
\
\
\

2. What was Alyce's problem at the Blunt cottage? How did she try to solve it? Why didn't her solutions work?

\
\
\
\

3. Judge Alyce's decision to send Matthew for the midwife. What would you have done in the same situation?

\
\
\
\

4. Why did Alyce decide to run away even though she liked her life in the village?

\
\
\
\

Vocabulary
Chapter Twelve: *The Inn*

Read each sentence. Then circle the most appropriate definition for the word printed in bold as it is used in that sentence.

1. The **bodice** of her dress was covered with lace.

    skirt   upper part   waist

2. Magister Reese completed work on an important **compendium.**

    summary   painting   composition

3. Alyce wanted "a full belly, a **contented** heart, and a place in this world."

    hopeful   satisfied   loving

4. The cat's **exertions** awakened Alyce from a sound sleep.

    exercises   noises   scratching

5. The rain fell **furiously** upon the rooftop.

    softly   quickly   fiercely

6. The workmen had to **hoist** heavy blocks of stone onto the patio.

    cut   lift   lower

7. The book's **intriguing** cover caught my eye.

    strange   colorful   interesting

8. Many wild animals are known to **prowl** after dark.

    howl   hunt   slumber

9. The **renowned** pianist appeared at a local contest.

    famous   novice   talented

10. Magister Reese was a **scholarly** man.

    scheming   quiet   learned

11. Alyce's job was to **scour** the tables at the inn.

    decorate   set   clean

12. The naughty boy **tantalized** his pet with some out-of-reach treats.

    teased   scared   helped

Answer the following questions in complete sentence form. Give examples from the story to support your response.

1. Alyce said, "I should just lie here in the rain until I die." Why didn't she?

____

____

____

____

2. How did Alyce obtain lodging at the inn? Compare her life at the inn to her life in the village? Which do you think was the better situation?

____

____

____

____

3. Name some descriptive words and phrases that the author used to create a word picture of Christmas at the inn.

____

____

____

____

4. Characterize Magister Reese. How did he help Alyce?

____

____

____

____

Vocabulary
Chapter Thirteen: *Visitors*

Use your dictionary to find a synonym and an antonym for each of the following vocabulary words.

VOCABULARY WORD	SYNONYM	ANTONYM
1. begrudge		
2. bold		
3. bonny		
4. comely		
5. earnest		
6. excessive		
7. greedy		
8. incompetence		
9. kneading		
10. swig		
11. undemanding		
12. wretched		

Write original sentences that describe characters or events that have occurred in the story. Use at least five vocabulary words from the first part of your activity in your sentences.

____

____

____

____

____

____

____

____

Comprehension and Discussion Questions
Chapter Thirteen: *Visitors*

Answer the following questions in complete sentence form. Give examples from the story to support your response.

1. Why was Jennet pleased with Alyce's work? What did Alyce do to help Jennet with her little "economies"?

____

____

____

____

2. What news caused Alyce to feel upset and to think badly of herself? Do you think it was her fault? Explain.

____

____

____

____

3. Explain how Will's unexpected visit cheered Alyce?

____

____

____

____

4. In what way did the midwife's evaluation of Alyce differ from Alyce's opinion of herself?

____

____

____

Vocabulary
Chapter Fourteen: *The Manor*

Use your dictionary to define the following words as they are used in this chapter. Then use each word in an original sentence

1. **abide:** ____

2. **cluttered:** ____

3. **coffin:** ____

4. **desolate:** ____

5. **flail:** ____

6. **frizzled:** ____

7. **hedgerose:** ____

8. **kirtle:** ____

9. **laburnum:** ____

10. **parsley:** ____

11. **sickles:** ____

12. **smithy:** ____

13. **suckle:** ____

14. **taunting:** ____

A Letter to Edward
If Alyce could write a letter to Edward telling about her life at the inn, what might she say to him? Use at least five vocabulary words from the first part of this activity to write such a letter.

Dear Edward,

____

____

____

____

____

____

Comprehension and Discussion Questions
Chapter Fourteen: *The Manor*

Answer the following questions in complete sentence form. Give examples from the story to support your response.

1. Analyze Alyce's need to see Edward again.

____

____

____

____

2. As Alyce journeyed to the manor, she did not look at Roger Mustard and Thomas the Stutterer. Explain the reason. Do you agree with her attitude? Why or why not?

____

____

____

____

3. What made Alyce exclaim, "Corpus bones! I might as well be asking the fence"?

____

____

____

____

4. How did Alyce finally overcome her frustration and learn Edward's whereabouts?

____

____

____

____

Vocabulary
Chapter Fifteen: *Edward*

Read each clue and find the answer in the box. Then use the letters above the numbered spaces to decipher the secret message.

bleating	mayhap	mortar	churn
abandon	puny	reassure	campaign
devotion	ewe	frail	speckled

1. to give up by leaving
$$\underline{\quad}_{1} \ \underline{\quad} \ \underline{\quad}_{7} \ \underline{\quad} \ \underline{\quad} \ \underline{\quad} \ \underline{\quad}$$

2. crying like a sheep
$$\underline{\quad} \ \underline{\quad}_{2} \ \underline{\quad}_{5} \ \underline{\quad} \ \underline{\quad} \ \underline{\quad} \ \underline{\quad} \ \underline{\quad}$$

3. weak; of inferior size
$$\underline{\quad}_{10} \ \underline{\quad} \ \underline{\quad} \ \underline{\quad}_{3}$$

4. container in which butter is made
$$\underline{\quad}_{4} \ \underline{\quad}_{6} \ \underline{\quad} \ \underline{\quad} \ \underline{\quad}$$

5. to restore confidence to
$$\underline{\quad} \ \underline{\quad} \ \underline{\quad}_{9} \ \underline{\quad}_{8} \ \underline{\quad} \ \underline{\quad} \ \underline{\quad}_{14}$$

6. physically weak
$$\underline{\quad} \ \underline{\quad} \ \underline{\quad}_{12} \ \underline{\quad}_{15} \ \underline{\quad}_{11}$$

7. series of acts to achieve an objective
$$\underline{\quad}_{13} \ \underline{\quad} \ \underline{\quad} \ \underline{\quad} \ \underline{\quad} \ \underline{\quad} \ \underline{\quad}_{16}$$

8. deep affection; loyalty
$$\underline{\quad}_{24} \ \underline{\quad} \ \underline{\quad} \ \underline{\quad} \ \underline{\quad}_{17} \ \underline{\quad} \ \underline{\quad} \ \underline{\quad}$$

9. perhaps
$$\underline{\quad} \ \underline{\quad} \ \underline{\quad} \ \underline{\quad}_{18} \ \underline{\quad} \ \underline{\quad}$$

10. female sheep
$$\underline{\quad}_{19} \ \underline{\quad}_{20} \ \underline{\quad}$$

11. dotted
$$\underline{\quad} \ \underline{\quad} \ \underline{\quad} \ \underline{\quad} \ \underline{\quad} \ \underline{\quad}_{23} \ \underline{\quad} \ \underline{\quad}$$

12. cement mixture
$$\underline{\quad} \ \underline{\quad}_{21} \ \underline{\quad}_{22} \ \underline{\quad} \ \underline{\quad} \ \underline{\quad}$$

$$\overline{\ 1\ } \ \overline{\ 2\ } \ \overline{\ 3\ } \ \overline{\ 4\ } \ \overline{\ 5\ } \qquad \overline{\ 6\ } \ \overline{\ 7\ } \ \overline{\ 8\ } \qquad \overline{\ 9\ } \qquad \overline{10} \ \overline{11} \ \overline{12} \ \overline{13} \ \overline{14}$$

$$\overline{15} \ \overline{16} \qquad \overline{17} \ \overline{18} \ \overline{19} \qquad \overline{20} \ \overline{21} \ \overline{22} \ \overline{23} \ \overline{24}$$

Comprehension and Discussion Questions
Chapter Fifteen: *Edward*

Answer the following questions in complete sentence form. Give examples from the story to support your response.

1. Compare Edward's real greeting in Chapter 15 with Alyce's imaginary version in Chapter 14.

____

____

____

____

2. Define Alyce's purpose in sending Edward to live in the manor. Judge if the purpose was accomplished. Cite examples to prove your point.

____

____

____

____

3. What unexpected discovery did Alyce make about herself? Predict how this might change her point of view.

____

____

____

____

4. Guess what might have happened if Alyce had taken Edward back to live with her.

____

____

____

____

Vocabulary
Chapter Sixteen: *The Baby*

Use your dictionary to define the following words as they are used in this chapter. Then use each word in an original sentence

1. **barren:** ____

2. **berate:** ____

3. **commenced:** ____

4. **compassion:** ____

5. **curiosity:** ____

6. **discontent:** ____

7. **hasten:** ____

8. **kneel:** ____

9. **obvious:** ____

10. **prosperous:** ____

11. **resounding:** ____

12. **transform:** ____

A Job Well Done

When Alyce successfully delivered the baby at the inn, she felt a great sense of accomplishment and pride in her achievement. Describe an accomplishment that made you proud of yourself. Use at least five vocabulary words from the first part of this activity in your writing.

Comprehension and Discussion Questions
Chapter Sixteen: *The Baby*

Answer the following questions in complete sentence form. Give examples from the story to support your response.

1. In what ways did Jennet help the newly arrived visitors? In what important way was Jennet unable to help?

____

____

____

____

2. Alyce had the opportunity to leave the inn during the noise and confusion. Why didn't she?

____

____

____

____

3. Explain why Alyce finally decided to take action.

____

____

____

4. Why was it significant that the birth occurred on the first day of June?

____

____

____

Vocabulary
Chapter Seventeen: *The Midwife's Apprentice*

Read each sentence. Then circle the most appropriate definition for the word printed in bold as it is used in that sentence.

1. My brother **coaxed** me into letting him borrow my new bike.

    forced   tricked   persuaded

2. When her dog ran away, Marla was filled with **despair.**

    confusion   hopelessness   anger

3. I spotted a tall **foxglove** standing near my garden fence.

    plant   animal   tree

4. The comet was **invisible** to the naked eye.

    attractive   tiny   unrevealed

5. They used **merchant** ships to sail to foreign lands.

    combat   cruise   commercial

6. Barbara was **moping** because she lost the contest.

    crying   sulking   yelling

7. Jennet **scowled** when Alyce said that she might leave the inn.

    approved   frowned   cried

8. The man seemed annoyed by the **surfeit** of advice he received.

    excess   lack   supression

9. A **morsel** of food was left on Tom's plate.

    a full serving   a generous helping   a small bite

10. The workers carefully covered the roof with **thatch.**

    tile   straw   slate

11. The ballet troupe danced **vigorously** across the stage.

    gracefully   clumsily   energetically

Comprehension and Discussion Questions
Chapter Seventeen: *The Midwife's Apprentice*

Answer the following questions in complete sentence form. Give examples from the story to support your response.

1. At the beginning of this chapter, Alyce was given three job choices. List those choices. Judge which of the three would suit her best. Which would you choose if you were Alyce?

____

____

____

____

2. How did Alyce finally reach a decision about her future? Evaluate her choice.

____

____

____

____

3. What happened to Alyce that was unexpected? In your opinion, was the midwife's reaction justified? Explain.

____

____

____

____

4. What lessons have you learned from reading this story that can be applied to your own life?

____

____

____

Spotlight Literary Skill
Figurative Language

The use of figurative language helps to enrich all types of writing. Karen Cushman used various types of figurative language to create mental pictures that make the dialogue and descriptions more vivid.

METAPHOR: A metaphor is a stated comparison between two dissimilar things without the use of "like" or "as."

"The forest was a green carpet."

SIMILE: A simile is a stated comparison between two dissimilar things. The word "like" or "as" is used to make the comparison.

"The memory was like a knife cutting into him."

PERSONIFICATION: Personification is the bestowing of human characteristics upon lifeless objects or abstract ideas.

"The day caught up with him and he slept."

Figures of Speech

Study the definitions of metaphor, simile, and personification. Then read the following excerpts from *The Midwife's Apprentice*. Tell which form of figurative language is being used. Explain in your own words what is being described.

1. "The blazing sun of Saint Swithin's morning dried the hay…and saw Beetle on her way…"
   (Chapter 5) ____

   ____

2. "She passed through the forest of bright booths with flags and pennants flying…"
   (Chapter 5) ____

   ____

3. "…and night prepared to yield to dawn…"
   (Chapter 16) ____

   ____

4. "The moon was as round and as white as a new cheese."
   (Chapter 16) ____

   ____

Find at least one more example of each type of figurative language in the story. Explain it in your own words. Also tell the chapter and page on which you found it.

METAPHOR:

SIMILE:

PERSONIFICATION:

Spotlight Literary Skill
Medieval to Modern

Through the years, the English language has undergone many changes. The words listed on this page were commonly used during the Middle Ages in England. Next to each "Old English" word write its modern counterpart. If you have trouble translating a word, try to find it in the story and use CONTEXT CLUES to help you figure out its meaning. We use context clues by looking at the familiar words around the new word. Those familiar words help us to understand how the new word is used in the sentence. It also helps to look at the sentences that come before and after the sentence with the new word. (Some of the following words were used in the Vocabulary Activities.)

WORD LIST

Olde	New	Olde	New
bade		gorm	
bedevil		How fare thee?	
bonny		I am sore afraid.	
breeches		lardy	
clodpole		mayhap	
comely		mistress	
daft		tot	
dally		truck	
fancy		wag	

Write a short conversation between two characters in the story. Use at least five Olde English words or expressions in your dialogue.

____

____

____

____

____

____

____

Spotlight Literary Skill
Historical Fiction

Historical fiction is a type of writing in which true facts are mixed with fiction. These imaginative stories often include real names, dates, and historical settings to make the tale seem more true to life. *The Midwife's Apprentice* is an example of historical fiction.

Fact or Fiction
Separate the fact from the fiction in this story. On the left, make a list of historically true facts. On the right, make a list of fictional occurrences.

<table>
<tr><td>

HISTORICAL FACTS

1. Some ballads were about highwaymen.

2. _______________

3. _______________

4. _______________

5. _______________

6. _______________

7. _______________

8. _______________

</td><td>

FICTIONAL FACTS

1. A ballad was sung about Hold-Your-Nose Billy.

2. _______________

3. _______________

4. _______________

5. _______________

6. _______________

7. _______________

8. _______________

</td></tr>
</table>

Creative-Writing Activity
Writing an Original Historical-Fiction Story

Choose a period of history in which to set your story. Your story might take place during the Age of Exploration, the Colonial Period, the Revolutionary War, or any other favorite period in history. First list at least ten historical facts about the period you have chosen. You may use a reference book to find out information about this period of time. Use these facts as well as knowledge you already have as background. Add many imaginative fictional facts to your story.

Historical Facts about __________________________

1. ____

2. ____

3. ____

4. ____

5. ____

6. ____

7. ____

8. ____

9. ____

10. ____

Draw an illustration for your story in the space below. Write your final story with all its details on another sheet (or sheets) of paper.

What's in a Name
Brat to Beetle to Alyce

It was the custom at the time in which this story was set to name a person according to some identifying characteristic: physical appearance, behavior, duties, occupation, pastime, or place of residence.

PART I: *Identifying Characteristics*

Listed below are some of the names from The Midwife's Apprentice. Determine how each person might have been named. Write the identifying characteristic—occupation, residence, duty, appearance, behavior, pastime, etc. — on the line opposite the name.

1. John at the Bridge __________________________________

2. Gob the Groom __________________________________

3. Will Russet __________________________________

4. Thomas at Bridge __________________________________

5. John Dark __________________________________

6. Jane Sharp __________________________________

7. Robert Weaver __________________________________

8. Thomas the Stutterer __________________________________

9. Steven the Fletcher __________________________________

10. Beetle (Dung Beetle) __________________________________

PART II: *Modern Names*

Can you think of family names that are common today that originated from an occupation or a place of residence? Think carefully. They are more common than you might at first realize. List your ideas in the space below.

Critic's Corner
Write a Book Review

Pretend that you are writing a review of *The Midwife's Apprentice* for the book-review section of your local newspaper. Your job is to provide information about the book and to evaluate its worth for your readers. Be sure to include the setting, plot, and characterization as well as your general opinion of the book. Among the topics you might want to discuss are the believability of the plot and characters, the suitability of the vocabulary and dialogue, and the writing style of the author.

TITLE OF THE BOOK: *The Midwife's Apprentice*

AUTHOR: Karen Cushman

SETTING

____

____

____

DESCRIPTION OF MAIN CHARACTER AND SUPPORTING CHARACTERS

____

____

____

____

SUMMARY OF PLOT

____

____

____

____

OPINION OF BOOK: Characterization, Interest of Plot, Believability, Dialogue, Etc.

____

____

____

____

Critic's Corner
Create a Poster

Create a poster to encourage other students in your school to read this novel.

Cooperative-Learning Activity
Compose a Ballad

A **ballad** is a type of narrative poetry. It is a story set to music. The most popular type of ballad has a four-line stanza. The second and fourth lines, which are shorter, usually rhyme. During the Middle Ages in England, minstrels traveled from town to town and from castle to castle performing their ballads. Some ballads were handed down from generation to generation. Sometimes the ballads were sung to accompany folk dances.

Along with members of your cooperative-learning group, compose a ballad based on the story of *The Midwife's Apprentice*. Perform it for your classmates. Write your ideas in the space below.

Post-Reading Activity
What Happened Next?

Alyce now knows her place in the world! She has made friends and has learned a valuable lesson. But what will happen to her in the future? What adventures await her? How will she handle another failure? Use your imagination to predict what will happen next. Write your thoughts in the form of a story.

Post-Reading Activity
Problem Solving

In this story, Alyce encountered many problems. Select two problem situations. Describe each problem and tell how you would have solved the problem differently.

PROBLEM #1:

____

____

How Alyce Solved the Problem:

____

____

____

My Solution:

____

____

____

PROBLEM #2:

____

____

How Alyce Solved the Problem:

____

____

____

My Solution:

____

____

More Post-Reading Activities

1. Learn more about the practice of midwifery in history and in present-day life. Call a local hospital for information about midwife services in your area. Prepare a report to share with the class.

2. Dramatize the story! Create a play, TV show, monologue, puppet show, or other type of drama to present to your classmates. Dress up in medieval costumes to represent story characters.

3. In the story, Alyce attends the Saint Swithin's Day Fair. Create a Medieval Fair in your classroom. Learn about the games, foods, and attractions that were popular at fairs in the Middle Ages.

4. Investigate life in the Middle Ages. Learn about the inhabitants of a manor house: the workers and the lord and lady. Create a tapestry or mural to show your findings.

5. Select two story characters to compare and contrast. First list the qualities or characteristics you wish to differentiate. Then chart your findings.

6. Many herbs were discussed in this novel. Make a list of them and tell how they were helpful in the story. Research the ways that herbs are used in medicine today to solve health problems.

7. Create a poster to encourage other students in your school to read this novel. Place your completed poster in the school library.

Crossword Puzzle
The Midwife's Apprentice

See how much you remember about *The Midwife's Apprentice*. Have fun!

ACROSS

1. Alyce had these to spend at the fair.
7. Giving human characteristics to objects or ideas.
9. Comparison of two unlike things using "like" or "as."
10. Magister Reese enjoyed eating them.
12. She did most of the work at the inn.
13. A midwife.
16. She told Alyce where Edward was.
17. Outhouse toilet.
19. Alyce's chosen career.
21. Magister Reese taught Alyce to do this.
23. Olde English word for "perhaps."
24. Alyce's first friend.
25. Alyce thought Runt needed a new one.
26. Owner of the inn.
28. Literary award this book won.
29. What Alyce used to be called.

DOWN

2. Alyce went there in the midwife's place.
3. Will's friend.
4. Beetle became one to the midwife.
5. What Beetle was called before Jane found her.
6. Author's first name.
8. Alyce and Purr found refuge here.
10. Wanted Alyce to deliver his mother's baby.
11. Will's cow.
14. Alyce saved him from drowning in the river.
15. Villagers thought the footprints were made by him.
18. Alyce visited him at the manor.
20. Author's last name.
22. Alyce was afraid to do this.
26. Alyce delivered her child safely.
27. What Edward used to be called.

Glossary of Literary Terms

Alliteration: Repetition of initial (beginning), sounds in 2 or more consecutive or neighboring words.

Analogy: A comparison based upon the resemblance in some particular ways between things that are otherwise unlike.

Anecdote: A short account of an interesting, amusing, or biographical occurrence.

Anticlimax: An event that is less important than what occurred before it.

Archaic language: Language that was once common in a particular historic period but which is no longer commonly used.

Cause and effect: The relationship in which one condition brings about another condition as a direct result. The result, or consequence, is called the effect.

Character development: The ways in which the author shows how a character changes as the story proceeds.

Characterization: The method used by the author to give readers information about a character; a description or representation of a person's qualities or peculiarities.

Classify: To arrange according to a category or trait.

Climax: The moment when the action in a story reaches its greatest conflict.

Compare and contrast: To examine the likenesses and differences of two people, ideas, or things. (*Contrast* emphasizes differences. *Compare* may focus on likenesses alone or on likenesses and differences.)

Conflict: The main source of drama and tension in a literary work; the discord between persons or forces that brings about dramatic action.

Connotation: Something suggested or implied, not actually stated.

Description: An account that gives the reader a mental image or picture of something.

Dialect: A form of language used in a certain geographic region; it is distinguished from the standard form of the language by pronunciation, grammar, and/or vocabulary.

Dialogue (dialog): The parts of a literary work that represent conversation.

Fact: A piece of information that can be proven or verified.

Figurative language: Description of one thing in terms usually used for something else. Simile and metaphor are examples of figurative language.

Flashback: The insertion of an earlier event into the normal chronological sequence of a narrative.

Foreshadowing: The use of clues to give readers a hint of events that will occur later on.

Historical fiction: Fiction represented in a setting true to the history of the time in which the story takes place.

Imagery: Language that appeals to the senses; the use of figures of speech or vivid descriptions to produce mental images.

Irony: The use of words to express the opposite of their literal meaning.

Legend: A story handed down from earlier times; its truth is popularly accepted but can't be verified.

Limerick: Humorous 5-lined poem with form *aabba*. Lines 1, 2 and 5 are longer than lines 3 and 4.

Metaphor: A figure of speech that compares two unlike things without the use of "like" or "as."

Mood: The feeling that the author creates for the reader.

Motivation: The reasons for the behavior of a character.

Narrative: The type of writing that tells a story.

Narrator: The character who tells the story.

Opinion: A personal point of view or belief.

Parody: Writing that ridicules or imitates something more serious.

Personification: Figure of speech in which an inanimate object or an abstract idea is given human characteristics.

Play: A literary work written in dialogue form and usually performed before an audience.

Plot: The arrangement or sequence of events in a story.

Point of view: The perspective from which a story is told.

Protagonist: The main character.

Pun: A play on words that are similar in sound but different in meaning.

Realistic fiction: True-to-life fiction; people, places, and happenings are similar to those in real life.

Resolution: Part of the plot (from climax on) where the main dramatic conflict is worked out.

Satire: A literary work that pokes fun at individual or societal weaknesses.

Sequencing: The placement of story elements in the order of their occurrence.

Setting: The time and place in which the story occurs.

Simile: A figure of speech that uses "like" or "as" to compare two unlike things.

Stereotype: A character whose personality traits represent a group rather than an individual.

Suspense: Quality that causes readers to wonder what will happen next.

Symbolism: The use of a thing, character, object, or idea to represent something else.

Synonyms: Words that are very similar in meaning.

Tall tale: An exaggerated story detailing unbelievable events.

Theme: The main idea of a literary work; the message the author wants to communicate, sometimes expressed as a generalization about life.

Tone: The quality or feeling conveyed by the work; the author's style or manner of expression.

ANSWERS

Chapter One: Vocabulary

1. dung	4. wimple	7. stench	10. unnourished	13. snug
2. fragrant	5. tormented	8. scavenged	11. bailiff	14. ill-used
3. heedless	6. apprentice	9. reeked	12. muck/rank	

Chapter One: Comprehension and Discussion Questions (Answers may vary.)

1. "She dreamed of nothing, for she hoped for nothing and expected nothing."
2. She knew the girl would do anything she asked in order to get food.
3. She reminded her of a dung beetle. Dung beetles form balls of dung on which they feed and in which they lay their eggs.
4. She thought it smelled better than the dung heap, but it was not as warm.

Chapter Two: Vocabulary

1. I	4. G	7. J	10. D	13. F
2. L	5. A	8. C	11. M	14. H
3. N	6. B	9. O	12. E	15. K

Chapter Two: Comprehension and Discussion Questions (Answers may vary.)

1. She didn't know any prayers, gentle words, or songs.
2. She kept walking away because she was scared. She returned because she knew the cat needed help.
3. She was basically kind; this was evident in her treatment of the mice. Also, she enjoyed watching the cat.
4. The midwife would not feed anyone who would not work.

Chapter Three: Vocabulary

PART I		PART II	
1. rows	5. coagulated	1. abandoned	5. harvesting
2. suffered	6. bottle	2. discourage	6. starting
3. buttercup	7. turn over	3. agreeing	7. insensitivity
4. sympathy		4. articulated	

Chapter Three: Comprehension and Discussion Questions (Answers may vary.)

1. She had borne 6 children, had gone to Mass, and had strong hands and clean fingernails.
2. Beetle provided cheap labor. She felt that she could take advantage of Beetle's ignorance. She thought that Beetle was too frightened and too stupid to represent any competition. Beetle was satisfied to have a place to sleep and two meals a day.
3. Jane mumbled to herself. Also, a pail of milk curdled as she passed.
4. She learned that she was smart enough to learn to recognize the syrups, powders, ointments, and herbs from their look and smell.

Chapter Four: Comprehension and Discussion Questions (Answers may vary.)

1. The baker was giving it to Jane.
2. Jane kept telling her she was going to do various errands, but she never took the things needed to carry out the errands.
3. She had never before been in such a luxurious dwelling.
4. The miller's wife was in labor and began to throw things at Beetle, who was trying to help her. A crowd of people gathered to see what was causing the commotion. "The summer sun, the...curious crowd, and the exertions of the...mother-to-be warmed the room to the point that Beetle felt like she was in Hell."

Chapter Five: Vocabulary

1. J	4. S	7. M	10. V	13. U	16. N	19. H	22. B
2. O	5. G	8. T	11. C	14. I	17. P	20. R	
3. A	6. Q	9. D	12. E	15. L	18. K	21. F	

Chapter Five: Comprehension and Discussion Questions (Answers may vary.)

1. She had gone to the other fairs as a beggar and wasn't in any condition to see what was going on.
2. Jane cared more about her appearance than usual. She "soaked herself in the millpond, dried her hair in the sun, and sharpened the pleats in her best wimple."
3. Jane broke her ankle. She sent Beetle to the fair to get the supplies she needed.
4. The merchant winked at her, complimented her, and gave her a fine comb; a man mistook her for a girl named Alyce, who could read. She decided to take the name Alyce.

                    The Midwife's Apprentice 53

Chapter Six: Comprehension and Discussion Questions (Answers may vary.)
1. Jane was upset because of her broken ankle and lost tooth; she told Alyce (Beetle) to get out of her sight.
2. The cat answered "purr" each time Alyce suggested a name to it.
3. While he and the other boys were teasing her, Will fell in the river. The boys ran away because they were afraid. Although Alyce, too, was frightened, she stayed and helped him. She saved him from drowning.
4. She thought she was not brave because she had been afraid. She tried to make light of what she had done.

Chapter Seven: Vocabulary
1. fetch   3. fared   5. delicate   7. idle   9. incautious   11. breeches   13. haymow
2. gluttony   4. paternosters   6. taunting   8. weasel   10. dewclaws   12. flung   14. wag

Chapter Seven: Comprehension and Discussion Questions (Answers may vary.)
1. They were superstitious. They were ready to believe it because of the birth of a 2-headed cow and a magpie that wouldn't leave the miller's barn. Alyce was not afraid of the night like the rest of the villagers; therefore, she could easily fool them. She carved wood blocks to look like hooves of an unknown beast.
2. Alyce took revenge on those who had tormented her; however, she did not have the "devil" visit the midwife. Perhaps she was grateful to the midwife despite the tauntings.
3. They were dealt with harshly. Thieves sometimes had their hands cut off. The miller, however, had only to stand in the rain with a millstone about his neck. Grommet had to spend the night praying and fasting. Sometimes people were branded; Wat was spared this punishment.
4. They washed up in another village. A woman found them and used them as fuel for her cooking fire.

Chapter Eight: Vocabulary
1. scrambled   3. parsnips   5. tart   7. accustomed   9. bounty
2. fermenting   4. nuzzling   6. gravel   8. cautiously   10. mellow

Chapter Eight: Comprehension and Discussion Questions (Answers may vary.)
1. She felt sorry for the cow because it was in so much pain.
2. In her excitement, she left the apples and basket behind.
3. They began to ask her advice. Sometimes they even gave her token payments for her help or advice.
4. She didn't realize how much she herself had actually learned. She thought of herself merely as an apprentice.

Chapter Nine: Vocabulary
1. ordered   3. respect   5. whimpering   7. trick   9. beat
2. moved about busily   4. swung   6. party-goers   8. comforted   10. poisonous snake

Chapter Nine: Comprehension and Discussion Questions (Answers may vary.)
1. She pretended to have a magic potion that would turn them into women.
2. Answers will vary.
3. She made up for her lack of knowledge by being caring, courteous, and hard working.
4. She felt pride and satisfaction. She expressed these feelings by smiling.

Chapter Ten: Vocabulary
1. abundant   4. pursued   7. manor   10. threshing   13. anise
2. tunic   5. sprawled   8. contractions   11. startled   14. leeks/mallow
3. huddled   6. reluctant   9. summoned   12. hermit   15. runt

Chapter Ten: Comprehension and Discussion Questions (Answers may vary.)
1. Alyce secretly observed the midwife deliver babies. She stored the observations in her heart and brain for future use.
2. The following are examples: an eggshell full of the juice of leeks and mallows will make labor quicker. Blood of a crane can make it easier. Birthwort roots and flowers can strengthen contractions. The midwife can shout into the birth passage, "Infant, come forward." Mouse ear and willow can stop bleeding. Tea made with anise, dill, and milkwort can help a nursing mother.
3. The boy described himself as a nobody. Alyce felt it would help him to be stronger and to gain a feeling of self-worth.
4. Alyce said Runt was not a suitable name for a boy. She went to the village to learn the king's name, which was Edward. Runt changed his name to Edward.

Chapter Eleven: Vocabulary
1. J   4. M   7. C   10. K   13. N
2. G   5. H   8. L   11. F   14. I
3. A   6. B   9. D   12. E   15. O

Chapter Eleven: Comprehension and Discussion Questions (Answers may vary.)
1. Matthew's mother was a sister of Joan, the Bailiff's wife. Alyce had delivered that baby safely when Jane hadn't given much hope of survival.
2. The baby would not come easily. Alyce rubbed, crooned, and fussed. She gave the mother a raspberry leaf and comfrey wine and she called the baby forth three times. She opened the windows and put out the fire. Alyce was too inexperienced.
3. Answers will vary.
4. Alyce only knew how to run away from unpleasantness. This had been her pattern in life. She lacked self-confidence.

Chapter Twelve: Vocabulary

1. upper part	3. satisfied	5. fiercely	7. interesting	9. famous	11. clean
2. summary	4. exercises	6. lift	8. hunt	10. learned	12. teased

Chapter Twelve: Comprehension and Discussion Questions (Answers may vary.)
1. Alyce had the will to live even though she thought she was "nothing." Her young body craved food and comfort, so she kept walking ahead.
2. Alyce traded her labor for food and bed at the inn. Answers will vary to the rest.
3. The following are some examples: holly and ivy hung from charred beams; ducks and geese turned on great skewers in the roaring fire until golden and juicy; the inn teemed with folk.
4. Magister Reese was a scholarly, intelligent man. He enjoyed writing. Although poor himself, he was kind to others. He never complained. By pretending to talk to the cat, he taught Alyce to read.

Chapter Thirteen: Vocabulary

1. refuse/offer	4. attractive/unattractive	7. stingy/generous	10. gulp/sip
2. fearless/timid	5. sincere/insincere	8. ability/competence	11. unassuming/demanding
3. pretty/ugly	6. extreme/inadequate	9. molding/separating	12. miserable/wonderful

Chapter Thirteen: Comprehension and Discussion Questions (Answers may vary.)
1. Alyce was strong, willing, and undemanding. She did what she was told. She helped Jennet with her little "economies" by overyeasting the bread, pretending to change to sheets, weighting the mugs, and not using beef or rabbit in the stew.
2. Edward was not seen at the manor. Alyce worried and thought herself too stupid to help the boy properly.
3. Will told her news of the village. He also advised her, "Just because you don't know everything don't mean you don't know nothing. Even Jane Midwife herself don't know everything.…"
4. Alyce thought she had failed. Jane thought that Alyce had given up. She wanted someone who would take a risk and, if she should fail, try again.

Chapter Fourteen: Comprehension and Discussion Questions (Answers may vary.)
1. Alyce watched Girtle nuzzle her calf. Alyce longed to see Edward again and nurture him. Alyce was lonely.
2. Alyce did not look at them because they brought back memories of her happy life in the village. It made her sad to think of what she had lost.
3. Nobody at the manor would give her an answer concerning Edward's whereabouts.
4. The cook told her. The cook liked Edward and was not reluctant to talk.

Chapter Fifteen: Vocabulary

1. abandon	4. churn	7. campaign	10. ewe
2. bleating	5. reassure	8. devotion	11. speckled
3. puny	6. frail	9. mayhap	12. mortar

Alyce has a place in the world

Chapter Fifteen: Comprehension and Discussion Questions (Answers may vary.)
1. In Chapter 14 Alyce had imagined him throwing his arms around her saying, "Alyce, you have not forgot me. Have you come to take me away." In Chapter 15 he ran to her and threw his arms around her. He said, "Alyce, you have not forgot me." These responses are similar.
2. Alyce wanted a safe, warm environment for Edward.
3. Alyce realized that she was pretty. During the washing of the sheep, she washed away the dirt on her body.
4. Answers will vary.

Chapter Sixteen: Comprehension and Discussion Questions (Answers may vary.)
1. Jennet told the man that his wife was pregnant. She sent the manservant to the midwife's house. She covered the woman with a cloak and told her noisy companions to leave. Jennet could not deliver the baby.
2. Alyce watched, but her sympathy, compassion, and curiosity kept her there.

3. Alyce argued with herself. She knew she had failed before and was afraid of failing again; however, she finally responded when the pregnant woman cried, "Help me!"
4. June is named for Juno, the Roman goddess of the moon, women, and childbirth.

Chapter Seventeen: Vocabulary
1. persuaded
2. hopelessness
3. plant
4. unrevealed
5. commercial
6. sulking
7. frowned
8. excess
9. a small bite
10. straw
11. energetically

Chapter Seventeen: Comprehension and Discussion Questions (Answers may vary.)
1. Her choices were to care for the merchant's son, to help care for Magister Reese's sister, and to continue to help out at the inn.
2. In her mind, Alyce recalled the joy and triumph she felt delivering a baby. She knew that this was her future place in life.
3. Jane refused to welcome her back.
4. Answers will vary.

Spotlight Literary Skill: Figurative Language
1. This is an example of personification. The sun is being personified. The author is describing the scene as Beetle leaves for the fair.
2. This is an example of metaphor. The fair is compared to a forest.
3. This is an example of personification. The night is given human qualities by saying that it would yield to dawn. It was almost dawn when Alyce delivered the baby.
4. This is an example of simile. The moon is compared to a new wheel of cheese. Alyce had just delivered the baby and went out into the night.

Medieval to Modern
bade: asked or told someone something
bedevil: to bother, annoy
bonny: pretty
breeches: short pants, like knickers
clodpole: idiot
comely: handsome, pretty
daft: silly, nonsensical
dally: to waste time
fancy: to like something

gorm: brain; idea
How fare thee?: How are you?
I am sore afraid: I am very afraid.
lardy: fat; overweight
mayhap: maybe
mistress: Mrs.
tot: a small measure
truck: business
wag: chatter; playfulness

Crossword Puzzle

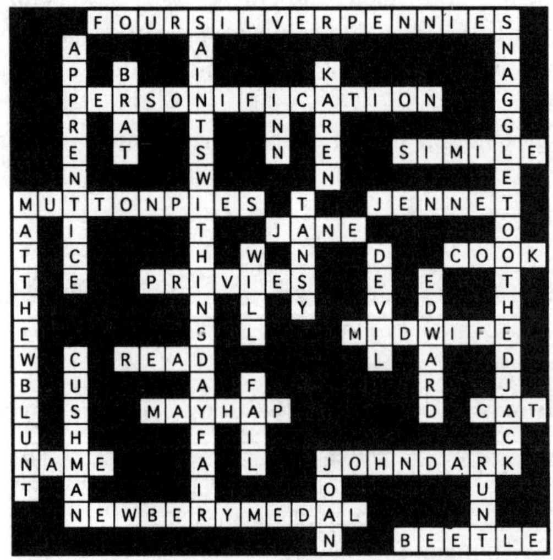

   © **Educational Impressions, Inc.**